Warne Gerrard Gu

CW00328164

PEAK DIS
WALKS FOR M

Clifford Thompson

30 circular walks with sketch maps

FREDERICK WARNE

FREDERICK WARNE
Penguin Books Ltd, 27 Wrights Lane, London W8 5TZ (Publishing and Editorial)
and Harmondsworth, Middlesex, England (Distribution and Warehouse)
Viking Penguin Inc., 40 West 23rd Street, New York, New York 10010, USA
Penguin Books Australia Ltd, Ringwood, Victoria, Australia
Penguin Books Canada Ltd, 2801 John Street, Markham, Ontario, Canada L3R 1B4
Penguin Books (NZ) Ltd, 182–190 Wairau Road, Auckland 10, New Zealand

First edition 1972
Second edition 1973
Reprinted 1975
Third edition 1975
Fourth edition 1976
Fifth edition 1978
Sixth edition 1979
Seventh edition 1982
Reprinted 1984, 1988

The front cover picture shows Alport Dale and is reproduced by courtesy
of the author who took the photograph.

Publishers' Note
While every care has been taken in the compilation of this book,
the publishers cannot accept responsibility for any inaccuracies.
But things may have changed since the book was published: paths
are sometimes diverted, a concrete bridge may replace a wooden
one, stiles disappear. Please let the publishers know if you
discover anything like this on your way.

The length of each walk in this book is given in miles and
kilometres, but within the text Imperial measurements are
quoted. It is useful to bear the following approximations
in mind: 5 miles = 8 kilometres, ½ mile = 805 metres,
1 metre = 39.4 inches.

Printed in Great Britain by
Cox & Wyman Ltd, Reading

Contents

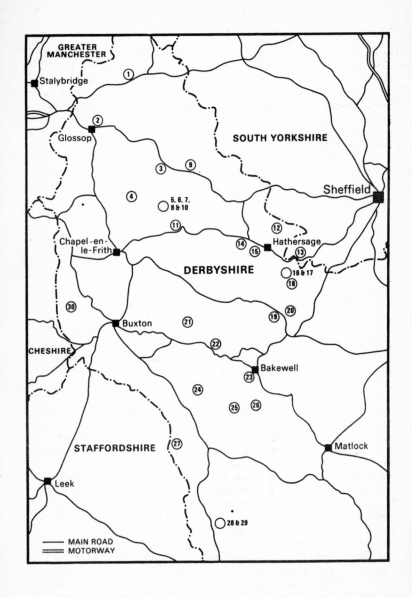

Introduction

The Peak District National Park is forty miles long, twenty five miles wide, covers 542 square miles and provides houses for 40,000 people who sell its farm produce and limestone beyond its boundaries. Over half is in Derbyshire and the rest is in Staffordshire, Cheshire, Greater Manchester and South and West Yorkshire. It is surrounded by cities and large towns, but has no large town of its own. There are no cathedrals, but there are several great country houses and well-preserved prehistoric sites.

The Peak District was designated a National Park in 1950 and as a consequence the Peak Park Planning Board was brought into being whose responsibility, then as now, is 'Preserving and enhancing the natural beauty of the area and of promoting its enjoyment by the public', to borrow the phrase from the National Parks and Access to the Countryside Act, 1949.

The Board is seen constantly to be active besides working ceaselessly in its quiet and unobtrusive way. It keeps a constant and jealous watch over its preserves, preventing indiscriminate industrialisation and erosion of the unique beauty of the area.

Evidence of the positive work of the Planning Board can be seen at Tideswell Dale where a derelict quarry has been converted into an attractive picnic area with tables, chairs, water and toilets. To the south is the Tissington Trail, a closed railway track of several miles which has been converted and signposted for public usage, together with another picnic area. There are the National Parks camp site at Edale, a site for touring caravans at Losehill Hall, near Castleton, and a series of scenic lay-bys at viewpoints with large car parks in the more popular areas.

On the other hand, the National Trust is an independent body which owns substantial parts in Dovedale, in Lyme Park, on Derwent Edge, Marsden Moor, Kinder Scout and Bleaklow plateau. It aims to preserve the natural beauty that exists and, where possible, puts no obstacle in the way of public access.

Information about the Peak National Park can be obtained by writing to the Planning Board's office at Aldern House, Baslow Road, Bakewell (please enclose a stamped addressed envelope) or by calling personally at the Information Centres at Buxton, Edale, Castleton and the latest addition in Bakewell.

The area is a network of paths and experience shows that the public is made welcome to use them. Rights of way used in this book have been checked as far as possible and the described walks steer clear of areas where the public has no agreed access. Don't be surprised, however, if, after August 12, you are diverted from some of the grouse moors. These are private lands which are normally open to the public by an access agreement between the National Park Board and the owners of the land. With the agreement of the owners, 76 square miles of these moors are patrolled by wardens to give help to visitors.

The walks should suit all tastes and are covered by the following 1:50 000 second series Ordnance Survey maps which should be studied before setting out.

No. 110 Sheffield and Huddersfield
No. 119 Buxton, Matlock and Dovedale

or more easily in the larger scale 1:25 000 outdoor leisure maps The Dark Peak and The White Peak.

Throughout the book grid references are given to locate the starting place of each walk. These are taken from the relevant Ordnance Survey map and for anyone not familiar with the grid system a study of the explanatory notes on any Ordnance Survey map is useful.

Readers are reminded that the *Country Code* should be observed at all times. This is printed below.

Country Code

Guard against all risks of fire.

Fasten all gates.

Keep dogs under proper control.

Keep to paths across farmland.

Avoid damaging fences, hedges and walls.

Leave no litter.

Safeguard water supplies.

Protect wild life, wild plants and trees.

Go carefully on country roads.

Respect the life of the countryside.

Longdendale

Longdendale carries the heavy traffic from the southern parts of South Yorkshire to Greater Manchester. High hills rise steeply from the reservoirs and all around is stark and forbidding. The two walks are on either side of the valley.

The walk to Black Hill is the longest in the book and starts from the valley itself. Bleaklow Head rises high from the other side of the valley and can be reached from Torside Clough, but here the walk starts from Old Glossop.

Go well prepared for bad weather on these hilly and moorland walks and take note of the following 'Hints on the Hills' published by the Peak National Park.

'Be sure to have strong footwear that grips. Protective and spare warm clothing are essential for all hill walking. For the more wild and pathless regions always take a map and compass, reserve food and first aid set. Think twice before going alone. Leave word of your intended route. Be sure of sufficient daylight. Take no risks with the weather—it can be as severe at 2000 feet as at 20,000 feet.'

Walk 1   Black Hill

10 miles (16 km)

The A628, a narrowish trunk road, carries the traffic from Sheffield to Manchester and roars all day. One and a half miles west of the now extinct Woodhead Inn and close to Torside reservoir, on a rough by-road, is the Crowden Youth Hostel, a fairly modern and very useful hiking centre in Longdendale. Start from the hostel (SK 074 993).

Continue along the hostel road through two gates and up the track.

The road, as such, does not last long and passes part of the Manchester water works and several signposts. When the climb starts, it is merely a rocky track.

Forward to the Pennine Way sign and turn right to the hills, keeping a metal fence, when it is reached, to the right.

From here on there is a path. At the start it is pure climbing, but soon there is a descent; not for long though, for high in front, to be climbed, are Laddow Rocks.

Continue on the path, crossing two main streams to a fork in the path, almost at the top of Laddow Rocks. By now the shooting range and wire fences will be behind. The first stream has a narrow bridge. The next stream has no bridge, but it is easy enough to cross. This is Oaken Clough. Just past Oaken Clough is a path bearing off to the

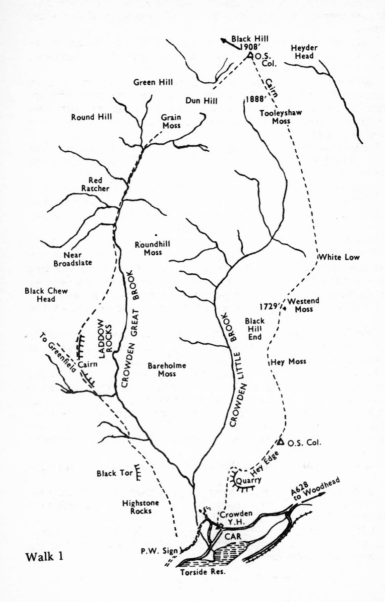

Walk 1

right. This is probably a good path to take in misty weather as it by-passes the rocks and meets the main path north of Laddow Rocks.

At the cairn near the top take the right hand fork and proceed on the path over the top of Laddow Rocks and descend gradually to the stream.

If the left fork had been taken, you would have landed up at Greenfield having walked across the moor, past Chew reservoir, down Chew Valley and past Dovestones reservoir.

Laddow Rocks, now past, is found to be a useful place for rock climbers. A head for heights is not essential, but for those who are troubled by high places, take the lower path, as the path over Laddow Rocks is fairly close to the rock face and causes imagination to work overtime.

Follow Crowden Great Brook upstream until it narrows to a stream at a noticeable fork. Continue along the path that leaves the water and climb up the hill.

Black Hill has been apparent for some time as has Holme Moss television mast to the right. The going now tends to be marshier than before, but near the top, the marsh, indeed most of the grass, disappears and is replaced by peat at the first of the cairns.

Follow the cairns to the triangulation column.

This is black peat and the hill is aptly named. In winter, this is a wet place with boots disappearing under the black sludge. This gets worse towards the column, a white obelisk of concrete with a desolate background. In summer, the going is over fairly hard ground.

Look for a cairn on the near horizon in a direction SSE and walk to it.

After the first hundred yards, the peat hardens into rocky ground, and more cairns, prior to the one visible from the column, appear, so consequently navigation is easier than it first appeared.

Look for more cairns and posts and follow them. Continue on the path, gradually bearing south and then SW up to Westend Moss.

The walk is on the highest part of the hill practically all the way back to Crowden. The going is in part marshy, but generally good and on a clear day there are extensive views, mainly in a westerly direction. Due south, of course, is Bleaklow Head, an ominous-looking sky-line.

At Westend Moss look for the OS column due south and head for it.

At the bottom of Westend Moss the path disappears. There is no path to the triangulation column, but below the hill is a path that returns to Crowden and is probably easier.

At the column, bear right and, keeping to the right of a quarry, scramble down the hillside to the path below. Make a beeline for Crowden across the fields.

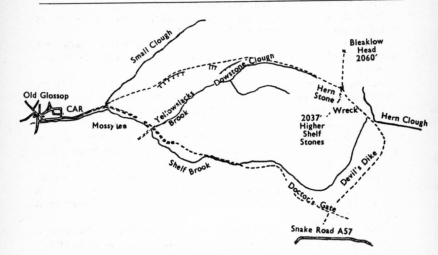

The walk starts from the Union Carbide factory in Old Glossop. There is car room at the eastern end of the works (SK 046 949). Old Glossop itself is a quaint village appearing to be completely, different from the town of Glossop.

Walk on the path that follows the stream until the first joining stream descending from the left is reached. Climb over a nearby ladder stile to the left to climb the hillside between a fence and a wall. After the fence, continue in the same direction up the steep hill ahead.

This is the steepest part of the climb. At the top over to the right can be seen Dowstone Clough, a fairly steep ravine. You are heading for the top of this stream.

Aim for the top of Dowstone Clough, keeping to the left of any rocks visible from the first vantage point and eventually reach the Clough before it descends steeply. Follow the path on the left bank until the stream disappears. Head for the large, solitary rock visible ahead.

This is a rock known as the Hern Stone. Away up the hill to the left can be seen the summit of Bleaklow Head with its few rocks.

If you want to go to Bleaklow Head make straight for the rocks on the sky-line. The best way is probably to keep to the right of a row of stakes that go from the Hern Stone to Bleaklow Head.

To find a wrecked Superfortress wartime bomber (with its attendant litter) go in the opposite direction and follow another line of stakes. At the last one, which is a double stake, look for the ordnance column. The remains of the bomber lie half-way between the stake and the column.

Continuing the walk: follow the path heading slightly east of south. This follows, at first, a dry stream bed.

When the stream bed enters a shallow valley, cross to the banking to follow the path that leaves the Clough.

Make sure you do not follow the stream, but keep a sharp look out from the Hern Stone for the path to be taken. Stakes may be seen on it.

Follow the path over the slight incline and descend a similar incline down a shallow, but wide, ditch called Devil's Dyke.

Once the top of the incline is reached look ahead for the Snake Road and attendant parked cars in scenic lay-bys.

When a prominent path is reached at a cairn, turn right to walk on Doctor's Gate. This is some two hundred yards before the road. Doctor's Gate is a Roman road that went from Glossop to Castleton.

Keep to this prominent path to descend to Shelf Brook below. Cross the stream by the wooden bridge and continue on the path gradually rising to a farm road. Bear left on the track and keep on it to Old Glossop.

Mossy Lea will be passed after descending to a weir in the stream. Later on, the ladder stile, originally climbed, will also be passed.

Kinder Scout

The majority of the walks in this section visit the wild heights of the plateau and these involve stiff climbs. In parts the going is arduous, so please read again 'Hints on the Hills' printed in the introduction to Longdendale.

Walk 3   Snake Path

7 miles (11 km)

About a quarter of a mile on the Ladybower side of the Snake Inn on the A57 there is a small lay-by on the north side of the road (SK 115 903). Park here.

Cross to the wall stile on the other side of the road and descend on the other side to the footbridge over the river. Turn downstream a short way to Fair Brook and take the path on the right hand bank.

The path shown on the OS map is quite indistinct on the ground and is probably not as easy to follow.

Keeping to the path, climb to the top.

The path generally keeps with the stream. Towards the top, the contours narrow and it is quite a scramble. If the path is not always distinct, head for the top of Fair Brook.

On reaching the plateau turn right and follow the well-defined path that keeps to the edge of 'The Edge'. When The Edge becomes less precipitous, head for the cairns that mark the descent of the Pennine Way from Kinder Scout.

These might not be readily recognisable, but keep in the same westerly direction until the path is reached.

Descend to the valley beneath Mill Hill.

Cross marshy ground.

Turn right and, keeping in the valley, look out for the path that will be on the left side of the stream down Snake Path.

There is no defined path to start with, but if the valley is kept to, the path and the stream should soon be seen.

Follow the path on the left bank all the way back to the A57.

This is most pleasant and sheltered with hills rising on both sides. For quite a while the path and stream wind through open country, but after you have passed a shooting lodge, you will come to, and walk through a plantation.

To reach the A57 when near it, cross the bridge over a joining river, turn right with the original stream for fifty yards or so, then turn sharp left up a path through the trees. A short walk downhill past the Snake Inn and back to the car.

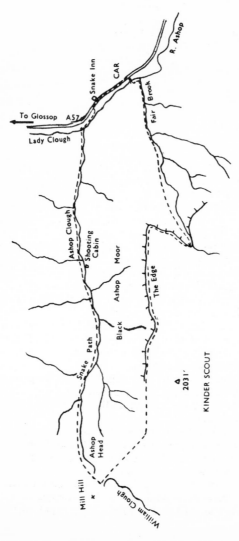

Walk 3

8 miles (12.5 km)

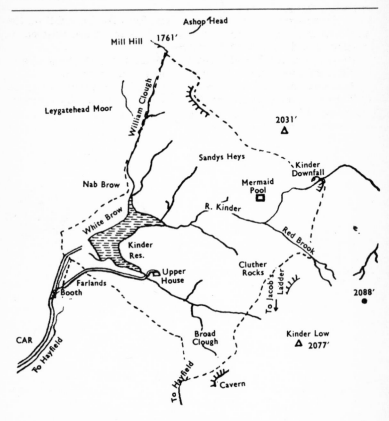

The turning at Hayfield for Kinder Reservoir is practically opposite the church and a narrow road goes directly to the reservoir. Park in the official car park about half a mile before Booth (SK 050 871).

Walk on the road in the same direction as far as the reservoir gates. Turn right off the road across the stream, then turn left on to a path to follow the stream as far as a bridge. Turn right and climb to the road, cross the road and continue in the same direction across the field, skirting a thick plantation. Follow the path as far as 'The Cavern'.

This is over farmland. The path is plain and is not all that straight. 'The Cavern' is reached when what looks like a dried up stream bed descends obliquely to cross the path. There are other paths from this junction going to Jacob's Ladder and Hayfield.

Take the path climbing east upwards and continue climbing to Kinder Downfall.

This can be seen for some time; a jumbled mass of rocks with a stream spraying over the edge.

Cross the stream and walk north west from the Downfall on the path that keeps to the edge. Continue until there is a steep descent to a signpost at the top of William Clough.

Beyond and above is Mill Hill and to the right, the Snake Path. Turn left and descend William Clough to the reservoir.

This is at times a scramble and the stream is crossed once or twice.

Take the path that climbs the hill to the right of the reservoir, then descend by a joining path to the reservoir head.

Return by the road to the car.

9 miles (14.5 km)

Leave the car in the official Edale car park close to the Edale railway station (SK 125 853).

Walk up the narrow lane, under the railway bridge, to Grindsbrook Booth.

The Information Bureau is passed on the way. This building not only houses information, but is the area rescue centre and well worth a visit.

Walk through the village to follow Pennine Way signs. At the entrance to a private house turn right to descend a path.

The route so far is well signposted.

Cross the stream by the wooden bridge, climb the bank and walk across the fields parallel to the river.

Note the four tracks both here and further up the walk and the manner in which they are being worn away by the tramping of countless feet.

Continue through the wood ahead to emerge at a stream joining Grindsbrook Clough. Cross the smaller stream and continue on the bank of the main stream, first on the right bank and later cross it to walk on the left bank.

This is an ascent all the way and the path gradually deteriorates.

When the main stream turns sharp right, continue forward up a steep and narrow defile to emerge on to the moors above. Bear slightly right to follow the narrow stream bed. At the top of the rise, after the stream bed has become a path, continue forward.

The direction is slightly to the right of a bank of rocks ahead called Crowden Tower.

When a recognisable stream is reached, turn right to walk by the stream.

The stream flows to Crowden Tower. At first the direction is due north, but gradually veers to the north west. The ground changes from hard ground to bog, especially when the stream disappears.

When the stream dwindles to nothing continue in the same direction. Look out for a group of rocks in the middle distance and head for them. This may take some doing as the rocks tend to merge into the background. They will eventually be passed.

A new stream source will soon be reached and this should be followed.

At first, no water, but later the stream proper begins and widens.

Continue by the stream and then river until Kinder Downfall is reached. This is a mass of rocks piled up from the valley below. Here are excellent views over Kinder Reservoir visible in the lower distance

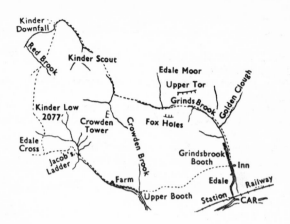

Walk 5

and Hayfield beyond.

Turn left to walk on the same contour on hard ground in a southerly direction. After crossing Red Brook, a recognisable defile, take the higher of two paths to start a slight ascent.

Ahead should just be seen an ordnance column. This will eventually be passed, the path bearing below it to its right.

At the top of the rise descend, bearing slightly right, to a broken down wall beyond a prominent path. Follow the wall to the right to descend a well-trodden path to a signpost at a joining path.

The new path rises from the right from Hayfield.

Turn left to descend the rocky path which gradually steepens to a signpost indicating the best path on which to continue. Descend on the left path to the Pack Horse Bridge at the foot of Jacob's Ladder. Cross the bridge and keep to the path that follows the stream to Upper Booth.

When the path reaches a farm, the way is on a more recognisable farm road.

At Upper Booth, the next group of buildings, turn left to follow the signpost to open country. This is through an open farmyard to turn right up a track which dwindles to a path on the approach to a stile. Climb over the stile, ascend a little way on a grass path. This is below the steep slopes below Kinder Scout.

Follow this contour, following the path, then descend over stiles and fields to Grindsbrook Booth, now visible. The last part is down a gully between a hedge on the left and the camp site on the right. At the village turn right, down the road, and return to the car.

17

7½ miles (12 km)

Park in the Edale car park near the station (SK 125 853).

Walk up the lane to the Old Nag's Head at Grindsbrook Booth. The inn dates back to 1577.

Take the stile on the left opposite the inn and walk up a narrow gully.

There is a signpost at the bottom before the stile. The gully is not too long and eventually opens out into a field.

At the footpath signpost marked 'Hayfield via Upper Booth and Jacob's Ladder' climb the stile and cross the field to another signpost. Keep to the signpost to the next stile and the one beyond that.

This is a walk up the field without path. Once over the last stile there is a path.

Keep to the path and walk to Upper Booth, ignoring a path that goes to Crowden Clough.

Upper Booth is a small village with a single road passing through.

Proceed up the road and then the path to Jacob's Ladder.

The road peters out shortly before Lee House Farm, the last farm before Jacob's Ladder. Once past the farm the going is on a firm path to the narrow pack horse bridge over the stream at the foot of Jacob's Ladder.

Take the right hand path and climb Jacob's Ladder. The going is steep until the next signpost is reached.

Continue on the path, eventually passing cairns, until another signpost is reached and where the path levels off and begins to descend to Hayfield.

Turn right up a fainter path to the rocks above. At the stone wall under the rocks turn right over the wall and walk generally east on the path as far as Fox Holes.

This is practically level although at first there is a slight ascent. There are fine views over Edale as the path is always close to the edge, as it were. Crowden Tower is what one might term a cemetery, a rock-strewn graveyard. We had competitions to identify the rocks which have assumed a variety of shapes. There was General de Gaulle, a pig, 'See no evil, hear no evil, speak no evil', and mother with child!

Just past Crowden Tower is the top of Crowden Brook, a precipitous ravine, which has not to be negotiated. Beyond is level ground with the path less distinct. However, the way is easy, for you are heading for the high hill of Fox Holes, which is to the right of the valley of Grinds Brook, almost *too* popular with ramblers.

At Fox Holes, turn south down the hill and then turn slightly left

18

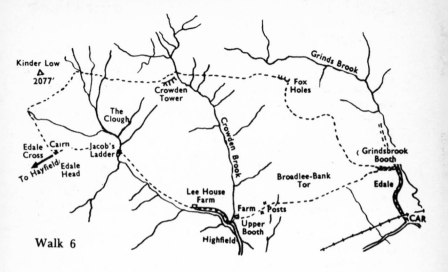

Walk 6

to the track at the other side of a wall. The track was used by the Edale peat diggers, who dug peat on Kinder Scout before the railway came to Edale. (Did peat digging stop because the railway brought coal, a superior fuel?) Descend by the track to the fields below and thus back to the car.

4 miles (6.5 km)

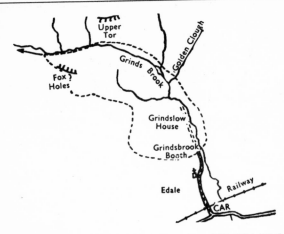

Park in the Edale car park near the station (SK 125 853).

Walk up the road past the church and Information Bureau, to the Old Nag's Head.

It might be worth calling at the Information Bureau as this walk is practically the 'Edale Nature Trail', literature about which can be bought at the bureau.

Continue past the Nag's Head up the lane which eventually goes to Grindslow House, but at a gate marked 'Private road' turn right to descend to the river and cross by the wooden bridge. Climb to the pastures on the other side of the river. Follow the path over the field, keeping parallel to the river. Continue on the path by the river until the stream turns sharp right.

It is a steady, but gradual ascent all the way. The way becomes less easy the higher the ground.

Climb forward up a narrow defile leaving the main stream.

This is quite a scramble. Now is the time to look back and gaze pityingly at the many who are sure to be following way down the path!

Turn left at the top and head for the highest point which is Fox Holes.

You seem now to be on top of the world! Below is Edale and beyond are the heights of Mam Tor.

Descend towards Edale on a faint path, if you can find it, to join a track beyond a stone wall visible from Fox Holes. Keeping to the track, descend to the fields below and back to the car.

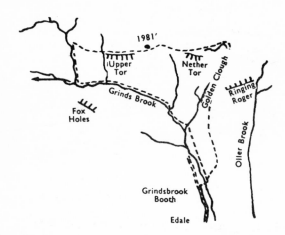

Park in the Edale car park near the station (SK 125 853).

Walk up the road to the Old Nag's Head and continue up the track that eventually reaches Grindslow House, to turn right at a gate marked 'Private'.

Descend the path and cross the bridge over the stream. Climb to the field above. Leave the path and climb the hill to the right to a large ladder stile high up on the hillside.

Head upwards on a made path and at its conclusion continue on a narrow path towards Golden Clough.

Climb the valley to the plateau of Kinder Scout.

A rough, steep climb, Ringing Roger means a detour but is worth it for the view of Edale valley.

Turn west and walk on a path round the rim of rocks until the main stream of Grinds Brook is reached.

There are other feeder streams, but when the path begins to bear north, scramble down the rocks to the stream.

Follow the stream downstream back to Edale.

At first there is no path, but when the stream turns sharp left the path begins and improves as the descent is made.

9 miles (15.5 km)

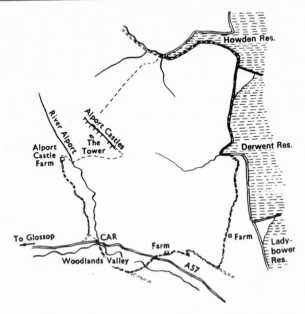

The walk starts at Alport Bridge, slightly east of the 15 miles mile-stone on the A57, two miles east of the Snake Inn (SK 141 896).

Take the stile on the northern side of the road at the footpath sign-post and climb the path to the white farm road above.

Directly to the north, on the eastern side of the valley ahead, can be seen the towering cliffs of Alport Castles, the immediate destination.

Continue north on the farm road as far as Alport Castles Farm, the only farm on the road. After following arrows through the farmyard, turn right and head for the river, crossing it by the bridge a few yards downstream. Walk upstream to the footpath signpost then climb the hill by a prominent path that ascends to the right hand side of Alport Castles above.

Near the top, bear slightly right then take the path that turns left beyond an old stone wall. Follow the path that keeps a wall to your left to emerge on the ground above the cliff.

This must have been a spectacular rock fall. Rising in solitary splendour in front of the cliff face is Alport Tower.

Follow the cliff path until a facing wall bars the way, then turn right to follow the path which at first crosses the moor, then descends through a plantation to a rough track below. Turn right and after a short walk join the metalled road at Howden Reservoir.

Take the road to the foot of Howden Reservoir and beyond to the zig-zag midway down Derwent Reservoir.

Fortunately there is a wide grass verge by the road side.

Leave the road by a track on the southern side of the zig-zag and ascend through the plantation. Keep to the track across the heights above Derwent Dale until several paths converge above Woodlands Valley. Take the more prominent path to the right that contours the hill, but which eventually descends in a series of zig-zags, at first, to the A57 below.

Cross the road to join a road descending to the valley bottoms, then ascend to join a track. Turn right and head for the main road and back to Alport Bridge.

The last part is on a section of the Roman road from Brough, near Hope to Melandra, near Glossop.

4 miles (6.5 km)

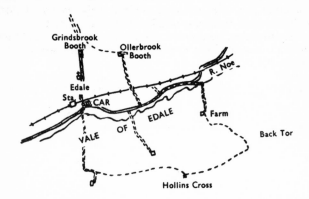

Park at Edale car park near the station (SK 125 853).

Out of the car park, turn right and walk on the road towards Barber Booth and turn left on the first lane at a signpost 'Public Footpath to Mam Tor and Castleton'.

The first destination can be seen from the car park. It is Hollins Cross. Look across and the highest point is Mam Tor. Look towards the left and the skyline descends. At its lowest point before it rises again can be seen several paths. This is Hollins Cross.

Proceed on the lane, over the river Noe and begin the ascent towards Mam Tor. Further up the road zig-zags and when the road eventually bears right, and where there are several gates, climb over a wooden stile on the left above a gate and take the grass path. Climb up a gradual slope in this direction and Hollins Cross is eventually reached.

From this point, as along the ridge east or west, are excellent views on either side. At Hollins Cross are a plaque and a map.

Turn left in an easterly direction and ascend the hill and then descend on the ridge keeping a stone wall to the left. Continue to the next dip at a stone stile.

Above looms the prominence of Back Tor, and beyond that the higher peak of Lose Hill.

Turn left at the stile and descend on a grass path gradually bearing left towards a mill and several houses in the valley below. Keep on this path, climbing over a stile and passing between holly trees to climb over a fence stile into a farmyard. Descend to the main road by the farm road. At the main road walk towards Edale to take the second turning right just prior to an old stone barn.

The mill, seen above, has been converted into flats, and the buildings, which probably housed the mill workers, are passed. The lane taken is a rough stone road and passes over the railway.

Proceed to Ollerbrook Booth, which is the small group of buildings ahead. Turn left into a farmyard through a gate, passing through another gate ahead. Fork right and walk over the fields.

Edale Church can be seen through the trees to the left.

Once over the fields, descend to the narrow footbridge to emerge at Grindsbrook Booth at the Old Nag's Head. Turn left and walk down the road back to the car park.

Hathersage

The scenery softens away from Kinder, but on one or two walks the moors still try to dominate the landscape. There is nothing as severe as Bleaklow Head and Kinder Scout; indeed there are one or two gentle strolls.

11 Mam Tor and Castleton
12 Stanage Edge (South)
13 Carl Wark
14 Shatton Moor
15 The River Derwent
between Bamford Station and Hathersage
16 Padley Gorge
17 Padley
18 Froggatt Edge, Curbar Edge
and River Derwent
19 The Goit
20 Baslow Edge

Walk 11   **Mam Tor and Castleton**

6 miles (9.5 km)

Before reaching the top of Winnats Pass, travelling east from Chapel-en-le-Frith, there is a signposted road to Edale. Park the car just beyond this, in the Mam Nick car park (SK 123 832).

Retrace your steps to the Edale road and ascend to its top. Descend to the first hairpin and take the path on the right.

Walking for the next half mile or so is under the shelter of Mam Tor. This peak can, of course, be climbed, but even if not, views over Kinder Scout are extensive, unless mist is present.

Continue on the path, first beneath Mam Tor, then on the ridge beyond to Hollins Cross.

Once Mam Tor is behind, there are good views from the ridge over Castleton. Hollins Cross is a country crossroads on the ridge where a number of very plain footpaths converge.

Leave the ridge and head for Castleton by the path on the right that descends towards the town.

The first part is by footpath which soon joins a rough farm track, which in turn becomes metalled, and eventually the road into Castleton is joined.

Walk south through Castleton to a T junction beyond the A625. This is really a left hand turn with a small road supplying the arm of the T.

Continue forward up the grass track beyond.

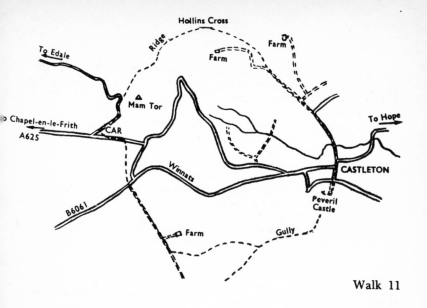

Walk 11

This is a minor canyon to start with; limestone on both sides. High above on the right is Peveril Castle, which you may find worth a visit.

Continue forward up the track to the top.

This continues for about two miles. Gradually the canyon opens out and at the top is open moorland. The walls are interesting if there are any left. They are smothered in fossils.

The path at times bends slightly left, but avoid any left branches or any sharp right turns and continue in the same general south-to-west direction to emerge on to a track near a farm.

Turn right along the track past the farm and keep this direction, crossing a metalled road, across a field back to the A625 and the car.

4 miles (6.5 km)

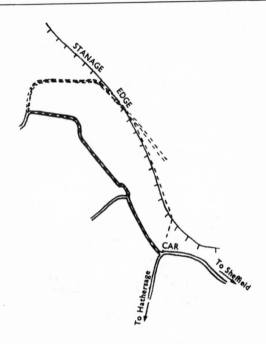

To reach the starting point of the walk, take the unclassified road that leaves the A625 in Hathersage at a sharp right hand bend and bear left up the hillside. This road winds over to Sheffield. At a T junction near Stanage Edge turn left and a short way down park the car in an official car park on the right hand side of the road (SK 242 832).

Retrace your steps back to the road T junction, then turn left on a pronounced path to walk to Stanage Edge. On reaching the top, walk north-west until a track crosses from above to below.

This is a high level walk, mainly on rock, affording fine views of Hathersage and beyond. The track is part of a network of Roman roads.

Descend the track to the road visible from the top. Turn left and walk back on the narrow and quiet road to the car park.

4 miles (6.5 km)

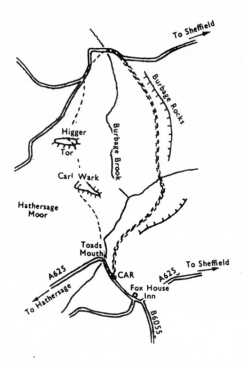

On the A625, about three miles south-east from Hathersage, is Toad's Mouth, a ninety-degree corner. Park the car on the left side of the road in one of the rough lay-bys (SK 263 806). As a matter of fact, there is a rock in the shape of a toad's head sticking out from the banking on the left side of the road.

Take the concrete road that leads towards Burbage Brook, going round the gate on the way. Keep to this road, which soon deteriorates to a hard baked surface, all the way past Burbage Rocks, to the road at the top of the valley.

To the left is the stream and beyond, the heights of Higger Tor and Carl Wark, both to be visited. To the immediate left, for most of the way, is what looks like a young plantation.

At the road, cross the bridge on the left, then take the track on the left to cut the road corner. When the road is once more reached take the first available path and head for Higger Tor rising in front.

This is not a steep climb, and it is worth it. From here are good views and a bird's eye view of Carl Wark.

Descend to Carl Wark.

This is an Iron Age fort dating back to pre-Roman times and probably used by the Brigantes, the northern tribe. Directly in front is the well-preserved wall, now leaning backwards and backed by an earth rampart. Follow the wall to the right and at the corner is the entrance, an incurved structure.

Take the path leading to the fort entrance and follow it all the way back to Toad's Mouth.

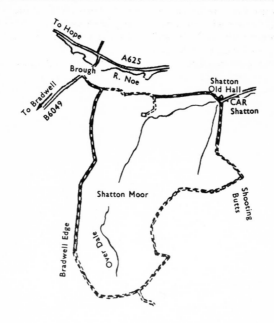

Travelling west on the A625 from Hathersage, after two miles a large
hotel, The Marquis of Granby, is passed. Shortly afterwards, on the
right, are the High Peak nurseries and almost immediately on the left
a narrow road bridge over a stream. This is the road to Shatton. Go
over the bridge and where the road widens further up, park the car
(SK 201 825).

Walk along the road in the same direction and turn right at
Shatton Old Hall on a narrow road. A short way on, a stream crosses
the road, but there is a footbridge. Proceed on this lane until it is
crossed by a gate.

Part of this lane is lined on both sides by very high hedges.

Turn right through the gate and continue forward on the grass
track.

The left turn goes to a farm and it is here the tarmac ceases.

At the next set of gates go forward through a gate to descend the

31

track that goes to Brough. Near the bottom, turn left on to an ascending road and climb the hill to the heights above, keeping to the road.

Over to the right can be seen Hope cement works and closer to, once a good height has been attained, there is a bird's eye view of Bradwell. Well over to the right is Mam Tor and beyond that, Kinder Scout.

Bear to the left along a walled track. Just beyond a signpost 'Public Bridleway to Shatton 1¾ miles', pass through a gate on to another walled track. Continue on the bridleway that skirts the hill and descend the hill. Just below a line of shooting butts turn left with the track to descend to Shatton.

Walk 15

6 miles (9.5 km)

The River Derwent between Bamford Station and Hathersage

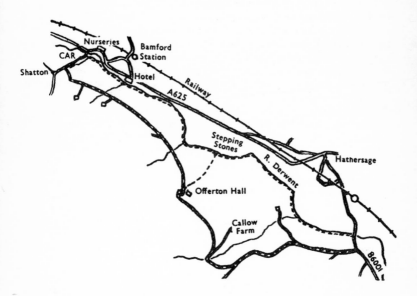

Travelling west on the A625 from Hathersage, after two miles a large hotel, The Marquis of Granby, is passed. Shortly afterwards, on the right, are the High Peak nurseries and almost immediately on the left a narrow road bridge over a stream. This is the road to Shatton. Go over the bridge and where the road widens further up, park the car (SK 201 825).

Walk up the road and take the first turn left.

This is a metalled road, but much narrower and is almost covered by the branches of trees on either side.

Walk along this road and generally in the same direction once the hedges have levelled out. At the first gate go straight forward on to a gravelled and grass track and similarly at the next gate. After passing over a small stream at a bend in the track, ascend by the track to Offerton Hall a series of buildings on either side of the track. The original hall is said to date back to the time of Henry IV.

Avoid the hall by taking the track that goes between the two sets of buildings to the right of the large archway. Once past the gate a few steps on, turn left on reaching another track.

33

Almost half a mile on this road, which is now a good surface for motoring, there is a path which, if taken, shortens the walk a little, but it is so overgrown that it may be missed completely. This goes to Callow Farm ahead and below. Once through the farmyard at the left hand side of the house the way is down the field and into Callow Wood to emerge on the road that joins the B6001.

If the described route is taken there are extensive views of Hathersage and beyond. The whole of Stanage Edge can be seen.

Walk along the road that gradually bears right, then sharp left over a stream to climb a slight incline to join the road that descends from Great Hucklow to the B6001 near Hathersage. Walk down this road to the B6001.

This has been mostly road work, but it is doubtful if there will be any traffic until the descending road is reached, as the way through is not suitable for cars.

At the B6001, opposite the Plough Inn, turn left and walk to the river bridge. Just before the bridge turn left through a stile to walk by the river for three miles.

There is a path all the way very close to the river and there is only one place which might make you pause. This is at a stile to a tin hut. Ignore it. Otherwise keep by the river until the next road is reached and to the left up the road should be the car. A good pointer to the nearness of the road is the back of The Marquis of Granby across the river.

To cut the walk in two, turn left down a track just before Offerton Hall to descend to the river at some stepping stones.

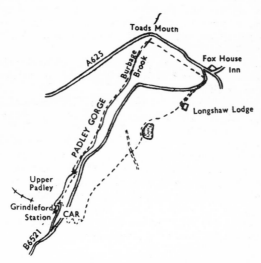

Park the car opposite or near the snack bar cum booking hall of Grindleford station, just off the B6521 (SK 250 788).

Keeping to the road walk a few yards down towards the river bridge. Before reaching this look for a squeezer stile round the corner of a wall on the right hand side, near a private garage. Pass into the wood and climb the hill on a faint path to the B6521 above, through another squeezer stile.

On this path, always bear right, ignoring all paths that turn left; there are a few.

A few yards up the road on the opposite side of the road, pass through another stile and immediately turn right on a faint path. Walk towards a shallow ravine and join a path. Almost immediately, turn left on to a path that zig-zags steeply up the hillside, bearing gradually left.

So far it has been all steep climbing, but well worth it once at the top because of the views over Hathersage and because there is no more climbing to be done.

Continue on the path to the left of a wall, now in the required direction towards Fox House Inn. When the path forks, either fork may be taken. The left fork passes round a quarry; the right fork first of all passes over a wooden ladder stile and over a field. In both cases, when a track is reached, cross it and ascend the incline on a faint path to join a path that skirts a pond.

If the track is taken, you will descend prematurely to the B6521 and face a half-mile road walk.

Walk on the path and pass in front of Longshaw Lodge and by the track to the B6521. Almost opposite, pass through another white gate similar to that at the end of the drive from the lodge, and walk down the plantation path to Burbage Brook, crossing the bridge at the bottom.

This is an extremely popular place for picnics and the head of Padley Gorge. The white gate at the top is the beginning of the Padley Gorge Nature Trail.

Walk downstream on the right hand path.

Although of open aspect at the top of the gorge, the stream soon becomes enclosed in thick foliage and is the gorge of its name. The path steepens.

As the path narrows, descend eventually by steps and cross the stream by a log bridge. Turn downstream by a faint path, ignoring other paths that disappear in all directions but the right way. Continue downstream, keeping close to the left bank until the Grindleford station road bridge is reached and, of course, your car.

3 miles (5 km)

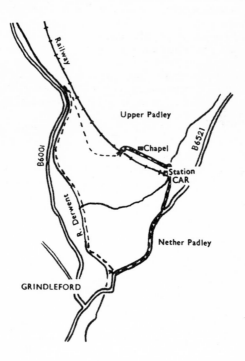

Park the car opposite or near the snack bar cum booking hall of Grindleford station, just off the B6521 (SK 250 788).

Walk up the station road to the B6521 and descend on this road to the river, near the church. Pass through a stile on the right hand side of the road and walk on the path through the fields until a converging path is reached.

The river is the Derwent. The converging path is where the railway line comes closest to the river. Before reaching here, a smaller stream is crossed called Burbage Brook, that descends Padley Gorge.

Take this converging path, as it were almost retracing your steps and ascend gradually towards the railway. Cross the railway by the bridge.

There are two bridges that can be crossed and either will do.

Over the first bridge walk up the grass track between two walls; when the left wall falls away the field opens out in front. Keep to the grass path that bears right with the wall to the track ahead. Turn right along and down the hard track to Padley Chapel.

There are houses immediately the track is reached and up the hill wooden chalets and bungalows. Padley Chapel is a well-preserved church dating back to the fifteenth century. Associated with Padley Hall, the church can be explored and its dark history is explained in a booklet.

Continue along the track to Grindleford station.

Walk 18

Froggatt Edge, Curbar Edge and River Derwent

6½ miles (10.5 km)

The walk starts in the Haywood National Trust car park, a quarter of a mile south of the Grouse Inn on the B6054 (SK 255 777).

Go to the end of the car park and turn left on to a path leading to the B6054. Turn right down the road that descends to Froggatt and turn left through a gate on to a fairly wide track.

This gate is equipped with a Water Board notice and near it an 'Open Country Boundary' notice.

Walk along this track, which is at first Froggatt Edge and then Curbar Edge, for two and a half miles to the next road.

After about three-quarters of a mile look out for a small stone circle. This dates back to the Bronze Age, roughly between 1000 and 1500 BC. Keep to the track all the way, although if it is a fine and clear day, trips to the very edge may well be in order to see the fine panoramic views of the Derwent Valley. It really is spectacular.

Almost at the road, climb a stile and walk down a wide track to the road. Turn right and walk down the road, but look out for a stile and a path on the left side of the road. Take this path to cut the long corner of the road and rejoin the road further down. Descend to Curbar, ignoring all turnings left or right. Cross the bridge at the main road and turn right along a narrower road that appears to go to a mill.

Continue to what looks like a converted church, near a caravan site. Go to the right of the building and continue walking parallel to the river, then away from it, across the fields.

In fact, the river is never joined on this stretch, although the weir near the bridge can be seen.

At the road bridge cross the road and take the stile. Walk down a short path, cross a footbridge and head for the river. Walk now by the river practically all the way to the next bridge, again on the left bank. The last little bit is on the edge of a field with a wood intervening between you and the river. Cross the river by the narrow road bridge into the village of Froggatt.

This is another of those delightful Derbyshire villages.

Turn left over the bridge and walk by the road until the road bends fairly sharply right.

On the right hand side of the road is an elevated pavement with a handrail.

Turn left on to a narrower road that is a dead end according to the road sign.

The road finishes after the last house not far from the main road.

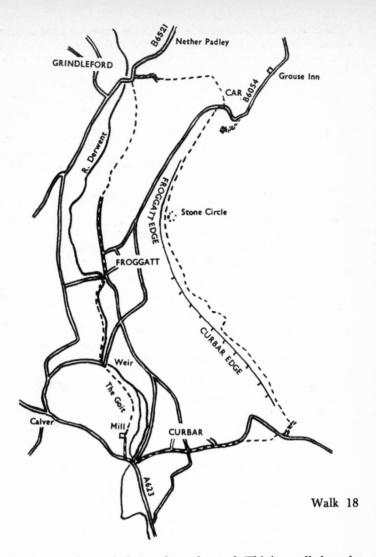

Walk 18

Continue on the track that replaces the road. This is a walled track with a pavement down the middle.

When the track ends in a field, bear right to a stile up a slight incline. At the stile follow the wall which is to your left. Continue in this direction on a path that keeps disappearing and at a noticeable fork in the path bear right. From now on keep to this path which becomes plainer.

In fact, in places there are paving stones.

Continue with the path that eventually emerges from the trees into a field and ahead you should see a garage and a church by the road side. Join the road and immediately turn right up a walled track to the right of the church.

On the left, after the church, are fairly new houses.

When the track reaches a narrow stream, beyond which are boarding kennels, climb a stile on the left to enter a wood. Take the path and begin the ascent.

At first the path is largely overgrown through little usage, perhaps because it is fairly steep. In places it completely disappears, but continue climbing in the one direction directly up the hillside through the wood.

When the path reaches a crossing path with a large stone slab with a metal cover, continue forward in the same direction as before. On the slab is engraved 'DVWB 1954'.

Continue climbing, now gradually bearing right, to join a wider grass path that goes from north to south. Turn right along it and look out for a path left that climbs to the car park.

3 miles (5 km)

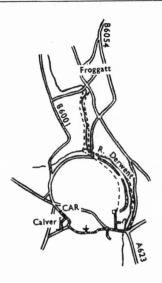

Park the car on a road near the traffic lights at Calver where five roads meet (SK 240 748). Actually, the walk could be just as easily started near the river, but Calver is another village to see on foot rather than through the windows of a car.

Walk down the village road to the bridge over the river Derwent, as opposed to walking on the A623.

Before reaching the river, turn left on a narrow road that leads to what looks like a converted church.

Near the building are sure to be caravans.

Go round the right of the building and walk parallel to the river across the fields.

The river is not joined on this stretch, although the weir near the next bridge can be seen.

At the road bridge, cross the road and take the stile. Walk down a short path, cross a footbridge and head for the river. Walk now by the river practically all the way to the next bridge, again on the west bank. The last little bit is on the edge of a field with a wood intervening between you and the river. Cross the river by the narrow road bridge into the village of Froggatt.

This is another village that is worth exploring though it does not take very long.

Once over the bridge, turn right and take the first stile along the road to descend to a path on the east bank of the river. Walk downstream to the next bridge. Cross the road and go through the stile.

Observe the notice about public access to private land.

Continue downstream on the path by the river to leave it through a stile a short distance before the next bridge. Continue to the bridge and return to the car.

3½ miles (5.5 km)

There is a road that descends steeply into Curbar from the east
passing between the joining of Curbar Edge and Baslow Edge. Park
the car at the beginning of the first right turn (SK 254 746). On the
opposite side of the road is a signpost, 'Footpath to Baslow via Gorse
Bank Farm'.

Start walking up the hill on the road. At the first bend go straight
forward through a stile and up the fields ahead with more stiles to
meet the road further up. Continue up the road to the tracks that
descend on either side of the road. Turn right and over a stile at the
'Boundary of Open Country' sign to walk along Baslow Edge.

This is misleading, for the broad path is not on the edge at all and
consequently there are no spectacular views.

On arriving at a single massive rock, turn left on a narrower path
to the stone cross ahead.

This is Wellington Monument, not very impressive; but from here
are excellent views forward over the Chatsworth estate. The house
itself can be seen, but not in any great detail owing to the distance.

Turn right and walk on the track that was joined at the monument
to join the previous track further on. Continue in this direction and
descend the hill by the track towards Baslow.

The track bears left. Beware of inviting paths to the right. You will eventually pass another 'Open Country' boundary post.

Further down, where the path forks, keep right on the obvious path. Ignore a stile on the right further down. Join the road at the houses below and turn right on the first road, which is Gorse Bank Lane.

This leads to Gorse Bank Farm, remembered from the first signpost. The houses in this area are quite distinctive. The turning is also marked by a solitary tree that has been made into a miniature traffic island.

Walk on the lane to Gorse Bank Farm and forward through a stile visible from the lane. You enter another walled lane which is extremely muddy. Fortunately there is a rough stone pavement.

At the end of the lane, cross a narrow field with trees to join a footpath with the signpost 'Baslow-Curbar'. At the next farm bear right to follow similar signposts. Round the farm turn left through a gate and across to the bottom corner of the field with its signpost. Walk along the path to the stile.

Over the stile, bear right to ascend a walled path on a gradual slope. Continue past a farm on the right and just beyond a small group of poplars.

At the end of the path join a grass track that leads to the Curbar road and the car.

Bakewell

The walks in this section are fairly similar to the last as far as the riverside strolls are concerned, but half the walking is over farm land. This is fine, but navigation is more difficult. There is usually a signpost to set you off and even finish a particular stretch, but in between there may be neither path nor guidance. Consequently in some cases, the indicated path goes a longer way round to make the route easier to follow.

Slacks are recommended, as some paths have been neglected and tend to be overgrown. There is nothing severe in this section.

Walk 21   Chee Dale

4½ miles (7 km)

Miller's Dale is a village comprising a sporadic collection of houses, a church and a pub. Opposite the church is a road leading to a café one mile downstream and the car can be left by the road side, close to the main road (SK 144 734). The fenced off old building near the river used to house a water wheel, but this has been removed.

Walk along the road westwards towards the high railway arches and at the other side at Dale Hotel turn right up a minor road to a gate marked 'Private Road'.

This is at the road bridge which passes over the river. The minor road winds up to Wormhill.

Go round the gate and over the stile at the signpost marked 'Public Footpath Chee Dale 1 Mile' to walk on the gravelled track by the river.

This is Chee Dale and the river is the river Wye. The private road is quite legal for walkers and foolish really for motorists. It keeps by the river and eventually peters out into a track and a path.

Walk by the river and at a narrow footbridge bear right to leave the river.

Until the bridge is almost reached, the way is thickly wooded. Half-way between Miller's Dale and the footbridge, the railway bridge crosses the river.

Follow the path to climb the hill; when it levels off continue on the pronounced path that climbs almost at once through a wood.

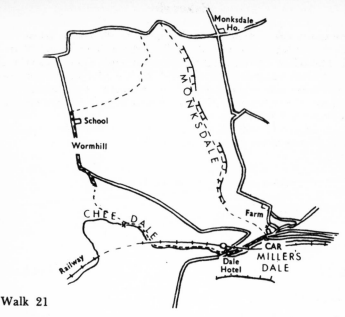

Walk 21

At first the path is stone and turf. Higher up there is a fine panoramic view of the whole valley.

Keep to the path to join a road.

This is the road ascending from Miller's Dale. Slightly downhill on the opposite side of the road is the entrance to Wormhill Head, an impressive mansion that can be seen from the road further up the hill.

Turn left and walk up the hill through the village of Wormhill, past the church, until the school is reached.

This is another quiet, straggling village with the hall, church and school on the right. The school is the prominent building about one hundred and fifty yards above the church.

Take the bridle path signposted to Tideswell Road opposite the telephone kiosk just past the school to join the old bridle path and keep on it until the next metalled road is reached.

The bridle path is at first a white, gravelled lane that later turns to battered turf. It has low walls at either side all the way as it twists and winds over the fields. Further on, the track deteriorates to a path that tends to become overgrown. The last hundred yards or so are downhill over a field.

Pass through the stile on to the road and walk to the bottom of the hill, climbing back into the same field opposite a notice board giving details of the National Nature Reserve. Walk across the field and enter Monksdale.

Not long ago Monksdale was overgrown, difficult to negotiate and a place to avoid. Now it has been opened and the undergrowth severely pruned. The valley is thickly wooded, but halfway down the dale opens out.

Follow the footpath that begins just inside the dale and keep to it as it more or less follows the bottom of the valley. When a wooden bridge is reached, cross to the other side of the narrow stream and continue down the valley. About two hundred yards before a row of cottages, climb a path up the hillside to the right, then descend to the road below after passing through a gate near another 'Conservancy' notice.

Before the valley was opened to the public a notice at the bottom of the dale, near the road, read 'Private property. Bull roaming dale. Survivors will be prosecuted for trespassing.'

3½ miles (5.5 km)

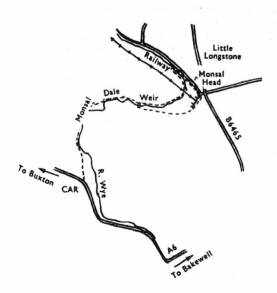

Monsal Dale begins about half-way between Ashford and Taddington on the busy A6. Opposite the signpost to the dale is an official car park where the car should be left (SK 170 706).

Go through the stile as directed by the signpost to Monsal Dale and follow the path downhill and over the stile at the bottom. Proceed on the path by the river.

Monsal Dale is a thickly wooded valley through which flows the river Wye. It is not a valley to rush through.

Continue past the iron bridge just below the weir, past the weir, on and under the old railway viaduct and round the bend of the river to the next iron footbridge.

No trains run over the viaduct as the railway has been closed. At the bridge beyond the viaduct there are notices to indicate that the next stretch of the river is private. This is made quite plain.

Cross the bridge and after passing through the gate ahead, turn right to ascend the path that climbs to Monsal Head.

This avoids the steep road that goes there. The climb is worth it because of the view and there are numerous seats from which to enjoy the view. From the top, looking forward, one sees the river Wye in the direction of Miller's Dale. To the left, the view is of Monsal Dale recently explored.

Take the signposted opening near the cottage and descend by the path to the river. This well-used path gradually descends to reach the river's edge near the weir.

Cross the footbridge below the weir and retrace your steps to the car.

5 miles (8 km)

Bakewell is a most attractive town. Whilst there, a visit to the Information Centre is worth while. Park in one of the town's car parks (SK 219 684).

One word of warning. On one part of the walk there are nettles close to the path and long trousers are advised.

Find the river Wye, and walking downstream from the road bridge, cross the river by the first footbridge.

It is very pleasant to eat sandwiches on this stretch provided the mallards don't eat them first.

Cross the field and the next bridge ahead. Turn right and walk along the narrow metalled road that runs parallel to the river.

It would by idyllic to follow the course of the river, but it winds and bends alarmingly and it is not possible anyway because of fences. Until the river is crossed further downstream, the path runs parallel, with the road occasionally visible. The metalled road peters out past the grandstand on the left. This is the site for the Bakewell Show held every August; reputedly the largest one-day show in the country.

When the road disappears, continue in the same direction through fields and over stiles to a narrow road that cuts across the path. Cross the road, over a stile and down a narrow path in the same direction.

For quite a while the boundary of Haddon Park will be followed, with its iron railings.

Continue on the path to cross the river and climb the incline to the A6 at a Bakewell footpath signpost. Turn left and walk along the road to the entrance to Haddon Hall. This impressive pile is clearly visible from the road.

Cross the road and take the gravelled bridle path signposted.

There is a fainter path that bears left, but keep to the right track that ascends the hill.

Keeping in this direction, walk first up the hill then over the fields to the barn and farm buildings and a signposted stile.

Eventually the gravelled track gives way to meadow land, and to the right two grass mounds can be seen, but keep to the wall on the left. Further up, a wall squeezer stile is reached with a signpost, probably without sign. The OS map shows another footpath crossing the one you are on, but this is overgrown. Keep the wall on the left all the way to the barn.

Turn sharp right and proceed along the old bridle path with the wall to your left until a road is reached. Walk along the road, past a road on the left, until the road visibly bends to the left. At this point pass through a stile and, taking the left and more obvious path, walk diagonally across the field.

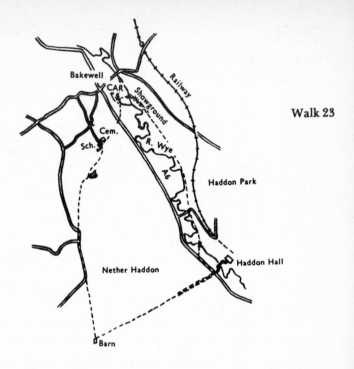

This path can be seen as a straight black line to a copse of trees over a second field. The path to the right heads directly for Haddon House and the A6 below.

When the trees are reached, take a stile near the bottom of a field and walk on the path to the wall which encloses a pond. Turn left with the path and follow the path, between walls, to the school above. Walk a little way on the road as far as the cemetery on the right. Just before the graveyard turn sharp right and walk down a narrow walled or hedged path to the houses below.

This descends to a housing estate and the A6. On the opposite side of the main road is a park, which can be walked through to reach the river again and return to the car.

6 miles (9.5 km)

The walk starts at a lay-by on the B5055 about 100 yards to the west of the entrance to Lathkill Dale (SK 156 664).

Walk up the hill into Monyash and just past the village green turn left at the crossroads heading south towards Ashbourne. After about a quarter of a mile where the road bends right at a de-restriction sign, continue forward on to a narrower road and almost immediately branch right at the next fork to walk on a walled track at first parallel to the road you have just left. Continue on this walled track past a farm, as far as the track goes.

The track surface gradually changes and at Summerhill Farm is merely a grass track. At the end of this section there is a choice of three gates.

Go through the gate directly ahead; turn left to walk with a wall on your left.

There is no path or track over this field. To the right, when walking, and on the horizon may be seen figures walking on raised mounds. This is your destination.

Keep in this direction across two more fields to a farm road.

Through the next gate a grass track is apparent and becomes more so through the next gate.

Turn right and at the road ahead turn right to walk to the farm within which is an ancient monument. The sign is 'Arbor Low'. Beyond the farm buildings is the monument.

Payment is made at the farm to enter the grounds. Arbor Low is a Bronze Age stone circle dating back to about 1700 BC. The stones are horizontal and are surrounded by two circular banks, the largest being about two hundred and fifty feet in diameter. Arbor Low is the best known of the Peak District prehistoric monuments. Nearby is Gib Hill, a round barrow. Indeed, the area abounds with these ancient mounds.

Return to the road, turn right and turn left down the farm track already walked upon. Instead of turning left over the fields continue on the white gravelled track past the first farm and on to the second farm.

After the first farm there is a sharp right bend in the track.

At the second farm, do not go forward to the farm buildings, but turn left up another track. At the end of the track, visible from the farm, turn right through a gate to follow the track that goes across a field in the direction of a ravine just visible.

This is the head of Lathkill Dale and the walk can be extended by about half a mile at the last farm where there is a notice to Lathkill Dale. This is a faint path that descends a narrow wooded ravine to

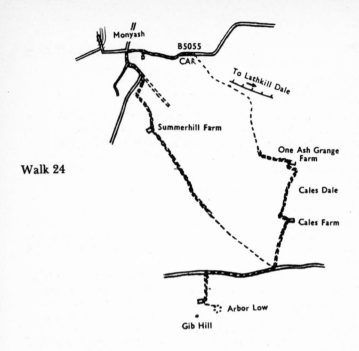

Walk 24

emerge in Lathkill Dale. After crossing the water turn left to walk along the path. Keep to the left at the next fork.

Almost at the edge of the ravine turn left with the track and descend to a gate and a signpost 'To the Dale'.

This is where the path from Lathkill Dale is joined.

Continue on this grass track to the road ahead, turn left and return to the car.

5 miles (8 km)

The parking spot is Moor Lane Picnic Site (SK 194 644). The nearest village is Youlgreave and if travelling east to west through Youlgreave take the first turning right which is about one mile beyond the village, then first right. About one hundred yards up the road keep right and look for the signpost to the picnic site at the next road junction.

Retrace your steps to the road junction about one hundred and fifty yards from the picnic site and cross into the field to take a footpath signposted 'Public Footpath Monyash 2' marked with a yellow arrow. Follow the path across the fields easily identified by the same waymarking on stiles and stakes until Callow Low Farm is reached.

Pass directly in front of the attractive farmhouse and through the gate beyond. Swing round the right-hand side of the barn ahead.

Descend obliquely left down the hill to what seems a limestone outcrop. Bear slightly right at these rocks and head directly for a farm that should now be visible ahead beyond a ravine.

You will not reach the farm, but go in that direction. The ground steepens and in front can be seen a gorge. To the right can be seen the top edge of Lathkill Dale.

Descend the field to the wall below.

Beyond is a thickly-wooded ravine falling steeply.

Turn right and walk by the wall to climb a wall stile.

Don't despair if it is not immediately visible. If you have aimed for the farm beyond the ravine, the stile will be well to the right.

Drop to the valley bottom by the narrow path that zig-zags down the hill. Continue on the path down the ravine to Lathkill Dale.

This will be on a slightly elevated position at the other side of the ravine. Lathkill Dale is about a quarter of a mile away.

Cross the water that is the beginning of the river Lathkill to join the prominent path. Turn right and begin the long descent to Lathkill Dale of about two miles. Keeping on the left bank of the river, continue on the path as far as Lathkill Lodge, a most attractive white house with stone outbuildings. This is at a narrow road.

Very soon the path becomes a track and remains so for the rest of the way down this thickly-wooded and truly charming dale. The route is a concession path and goes through a National Nature Reserve.

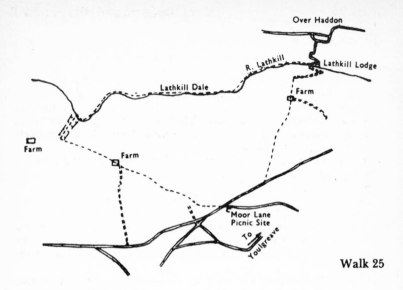

Walk 25

At the lodge turn right and cross the water at the stepping stones with handrails, then take the track up the hill to the left. At the first bend go with the track as it heads up the hill, now in the opposite direction.

Better views of Over Haddon can be gained as the ascent is made. This is the village on the opposite side of the valley.

At the end of the track pass into a field through a gate and cross the field to the farm on the left. Find your way to the opposite side of the farm and look for two signposts 'Footpath to Youlgreave' and 'Footpath to Middleton'. Take the latter and a path that bears right with a wall. Proceed by the wall to an open gateway and a well in the wall. Leave the wall and head for a gate in a facing wall one hundred yards away, bearing slightly left. Pass through the gate and turn left along the wall side.

Field navigation is difficult if the footpaths are not kept clear and properly signposted. This is a typical example.

Keep to the wall until the road wall is reached. Turn right and follow the road wall to the stile and attendant signpost 'Footpath to Over Haddon'. Pass into the road; turn right and walk to the first road junction, which is where you started.

4½ miles (7 km)

Alport is a small village at the junction of the river Bradford with the river Lathkill, both soon to join the river Wye. The village is about a mile east of Youlgreave and from the north is reached from the A6, 2½ miles south-east of Bakewell. There is a bit of spare ground on the right hand side of the road just leaving Alport for Youlgreave. Leave the car here (SK 220 646).

Cross the road to the signpost 'Footpath to Middleton by Youlgreave' and follow the directions to walk for a few yards on the right hand bank but then over the river to the left bank.

River is a rather pretentious word for the quiet stream. The path is gravelled and winds with the river.

Continue on the track passing a pack horse bridge to cross the river at the next road bridge. Take the path on the other side of the river, a path which after a short while gradually rises to the village above.

This is Youlgreave. The path joins a street. Proceed to the main road at a church on the corner. Turn right, then a few yards down the road turn left up a narrower road. The road bends left, right, then left again.

After walking up the narrow road to the second left bend turn off the road on to a walled track at a signpost 'Footpath to Over Haddon'. Keep on it to the track's conclusion then continue in the same direction over a field keeping a wall to the left until the road is reached.

There is a signpost at the road pointing back to the track you have just left. It is 'Footpath to Youlgreave'. Before this, pass through a gap in the wall and join the road through a stile.

Turn right and walk to the signpost at the other side. It says 'Footpath to Over Haddon'. Pass through the stile into the field beyond and descend the field to the farm below.

There is no visible path here, but follow the direction of the signpost. At the entrance to the farm are two signposts in two directions back up the hill: 'Footpath to Youlgreave' and 'Footpath to Middleton'.

Find your way through the farm and pass through a gate into the field at the other side of the farm. Walk across the field to trees and on reaching the wall in front of the trees turn right to pass through another gate on to a track. Take the long descent. Turn left at the hairpin bend and descend to the valley at the handrailed stepping stones opposite Lathkill Lodge.

Glimpses of Over Haddon can be seen through the trees on the way down. This is a village high on the opposite hillside.

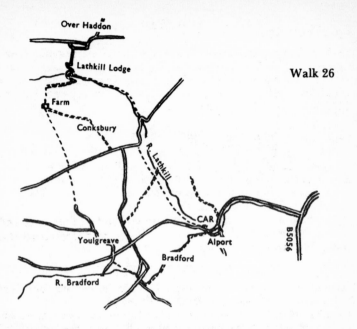

Cross by the stones and turn down the path, at Lathkill Lodge, signposted 'Footpath to Congreave' and proceed down Lathkill Dale keeping to the left bank of the river.

There is now a walk by the river Lathkill of about a mile and at the lower reaches the river descends in a series of weirs. These originate from attempts to improve the sport of fishing for the gentlemen of the nineteenth century. From Lathkill Lodge downwards is part of the Lathkill Nature Trail about which an informative leaflet is published by the Peak Park Planning Board.

On reaching the road bridge turn right and climb the hill to pass through the first available stile into the field on the left.

It seems a pity to leave the river, but this is private land and the division between private property and public access is made quite plain by the fencing at the other side of the wall.

Walk along the path, keeping the wire fence to the left all the way back to Alport and the car.

There are tantalising glimpses of the river well over to the left but it can only be reached at one point, where a track crosses the path and proceeds to an old stone bridge over the river. This, however, is a detour, for the path continues in a reasonably straight line over stiles from the bridge near Conksbury to Alport.

58

South West

The Manifold valley, Dovedale and Tissington are popular tourist attractions. Dovedale, in particular, is a favourite with those who like to wander along the bank of a delightful river in a beautiful valley. A car park has been provided at the lower end of the dale and there is a footpath for several miles upstream.

Walk 27   **Biggin Dale, Wolfscote Dale**
                                              and Beresford Dale
6 miles (9.5 km)

Hartington is a small market town with old houses and buildings. Park somewhere in the centre (SK 128 604).

Look for the church, which is situated behind the main street, and turn off the street on to a narrow road that almost immediately bends left by the Methodist chapel. Continue to the YHA hostel and three hundred yards past the hostel turn right on a small earthen track.

The YHA hostel is Hartington Hall, built in 1611.

Proceed on this track, ignoring left and right turns, until a road is joined.

The last quarter of a mile is rather overgrown with grass.

Turn right and just before the road forks turn right down a footpath bearing a signpost 'Public Footpath to Biggin Dale'.

This is a dry valley, hardly used, it would seem from the absence of litter usually associated with popular paths.

Continue forward down the bottom of the valley. At the next signpost go forward as directed. After another quarter of a mile, when there is a choice of left or right, turn right.

This is at a T junction in the valley. The path seems to take the left turn, but this has been made by people walking in the opposite direction. The reason will probably become obvious further down.

Continue down the bottom of the valley to join the river Dove at the foot of Wolfscote Dale.

Part of the way is through a thickly wooded area, otherwise the sides of the valley rise steeply, offering no alternative route.

At the river, turn right and walk upstream until the path no longer continues on the right bank of the river, but leads to a footbridge.

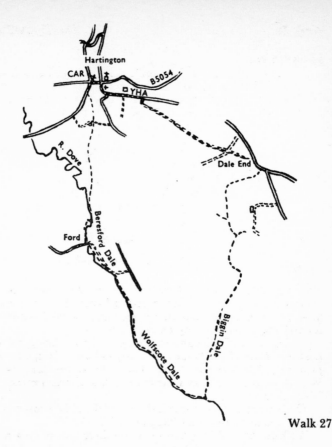

Walk 27

Just before the bridge is a well-preserved keyhole stile standing all alone. Nearby is a ford, leading to an overgrown track.

Over the bridge turn right and walk up the left bank to the next footbridge, which is crossed.

Again, there appears to be no access forward.

Walk on the path up the right bank and follow it as it leaves the river for the fields. The river is completely left behind.

Proceed on this grass path until progress ahead is barred by a gate with a small barn to its left. Bear right before reaching the gate to squeeze through a stile into a walled track. Opposite are two stiles close together. Take the right stile to walk the last bit into Hartington.

The path leaves the field at a petrol filling station.

3 miles (5 km)

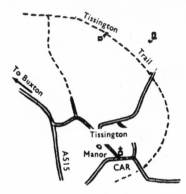

The Tissington Trail follows the former Ashbourne to Buxton railway and extends from Ashbourne to Parsley Hay. The rails along most of this section have been removed and the trail is now suitable for walking or horse riding on grass and clay.

Tissington itself is famous in the Peak District, being noted for its neatness. Most of the houses are fairly old and Tissington Manor is Jacobean. Folk lore has it that Tissington started the tradition of Well Blessing in the Peak District in 1350 as thanks for escaping the Black Death.

The Tissington picnic area is the site of the old station and is south of the village behind the village pond (SK 178 521).

Walk on the trail in a north-easterly direction, passing under the short tunnel ahead and two more bridges. After the third bridge, and before entering a cutting visible ahead, turn left into a field through a gate at a signpost marked 'Footpath to Tissington'.

This is an official Tissington Trail signpost as are others seen earlier. Unfortunately, although the posts set you off in the right direction, you have to find your own way after leaving the trail.

Bear right across the field to the far corner and walk up a walled track which is overgrown. Beyond, cross a field with the wall to the right and along another overgrown walled path. Cross the field to the farm road ahead, with the wall to your right, passing through one gateway on the way. Walk on the short farm lane to the road which enters Tissington from the A515 Buxton to Ashbourne road.

There is no well-kept footpath and it is a matter of guesswork which is the right way.

Walk through Tissington back to the car.

61

2 miles (3 km)

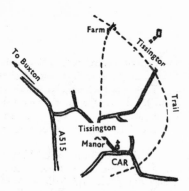

Leave the car as before, at the old Tissington station, now a picnic site on the Tissington Trail (SK 178 521).

Walk in a north-easterly direction under the first short tunnel, under the next bridge, but just before the next bridge turn right off the trail at a trail signpost marked 'Footpath to Tissington'. Climb up the banking and take the path that runs parallel to the trail as far as the bridge.

Look out for nettles on this stretch. The path tends to be overgrown.

Cross the railway by the bridge into the farmyard beyond through a gate. Proceed up the field directly ahead to find a narrow stile in the crossing wall at the top of the rise. Keeping in the same direction, pass through two more stiles, then keeping to the left of four tall trees, reach the brow of the hill. Follow the stiles down the hill to emerge into Tissington at the Post Office.

The stiles should be visible ahead, which is always a comfort. Any electric fences in the way will have to be negotiated.

Goyt Valley

This is at the extreme west of the Peak District in the area that juts out towards the Cheshire plain. The walk is by a yachting reservoir, incorporates part of a nature trail and follows a county boundary.

Walk 30   **The Goyt Valley**

6 miles (9.5 km)

The Goyt Valley experiment was started in 1970, continued in 1971 and has been reviewed from time to time. The idea was the control of traffic through the valley. This was achieved by providing a minibus service on valley roads and by preventing non-essential traffic from entering the area. The scheme now only operates on set days; at other times cars are permitted to park in specified places in the valley.

The walk starts in the valley bottom near Errwood reservoir (SK 014 751). Look for a signpost 'Pym Chair and Goytsclough Quarry' above the Errwood car park and follow its direction to a white post labelled 'One'. Climb over the wall and climb up through the wood. Once through the wood and over another wall enter a field at a white post identical to the first post. Follow the track up the hill to the next white post visible from the last. Continue up the path past a broken wall to the final white post with 'One' on it.

Looking back, the valley opens out, but the best views cannot be seen until the top is reached.

Continue up the grass track, now by a wall on the right, to pass a signpost to Errwood Hall.

This points down a valley to the old mansion which is hidden in the trees below. (Alternatively, you could have reached your present position through the trees by taking the path from the reservoir to Errwood Hall and continuing up the wooded path.)

Keep to the path with the wall on the right as far as the next signpost and turn right to follow the direction 'Pym Chair'. Walk on a narrower and rougher path, first descending and then ascending with a wall to your left. At the top of the slope, the wall turns sharp right as does the path. At the other side of the facing wall is the Ordnance column.

Now is the time to look round, for from here I estimate it is possible to see seven counties, most of them being to the west. In a west to south-westerly direction are the shadows of what must be Welsh mountains. To the north-west is Stockport and beyond that Manchester. An occasional aeroplane can be seen landing at

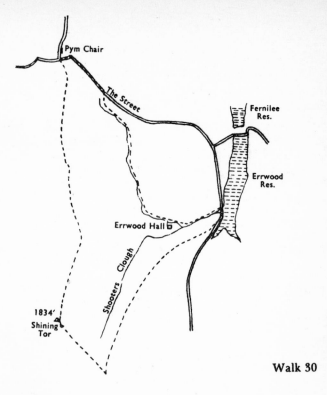

Walk 30

Manchester Airport. Over to the east are the Derbyshire hills with the black mass of Kinder Scout dominating the north-eastern skyline. Indeterminate views can be seen to north and south. All in all, a full, circular, panoramic view; one of the best available.

Walk on the path, now almost due north with the wall on your left, until Pym Chair is reached at a road ascending steeply from the reservoirs.

When the buses are running to Pym Chair they turn round at the small car park at the top of the hill. It may be worth while reversing the walk by riding to Pym Chair and walking on the ridge in the opposite direction, to avoid the long climb from the reservoirs.

Walk down the road to a signpost on the right labelled 'Errwood Hall'. Take the path that heads for a wooded valley.

Ahead can be seen the long ascent recently made from the reservoir.

At the bend and forward is a hill and over this are the ruins of Errwood Hall, which is part of a nature trail from the picnic area by the reservoir.

64